Contents

I like this page best.

What is Scratch?

A computer hasn't got a clever brain like you, so everything you want it to do must be broken down into lists of simple instructions called programs. Giving instructions to the computer is known as programming, or coding.

What you'll learn:
• To do tasks, computers need simple instructions called programs
• Scratch is a great place to start programming
• What the ingredients of a Scratch project are

What does a computer understand?

Instructions for computers have to be written following special rules and using only words the computer understands. These words and rules make up a "programming language". There are lots of different programming languages. Many have funny names, such as JavaScript, C++, and Python.

A program is a list of instructions for the computer

What is Scratch?

Scratch is a computer programming language that's easy for beginners to use. In Scratch, programs are made by joining together coloured blocks using the mouse. These groups of blocks (called scripts) tell characters on the screen (called sprites) what to do. Scratch is free, safe, and fun to experiment with.

The blocks fit together like jigsaw pieces

Scratch Projects

With Scratch, you can make your own interactive stories, animations, games, music, and art. Scratch has large collections (or "libraries") of cool graphics and fun sounds you can play around with. Let your imagination run riot – you'll soon pick up the coding skills you need!

We can make lots of sounds!

Carol Vorderman

Coding with Scratch Made Easy

Author and Consultant Dr Jon Woodcock

DK

Written by
Dr Jon Woodcock
Editor Steve Setford
Designer Peter Radcliffe
Publisher Laura Buller
Art Director Martin Wilson
Jacket Designers Emma Hobson, Charlotte Jennings
Producer, Pre-Production Francesca Wardell
Producer Srijana Gurung
Publishing Director Sophie Mitchell

First published in Great Britain in 2015
by Dorling Kindersley Limited
80 Strand, London WC2R 0RL

A CIP catalogue record for this book
is available from the British Library.
ISBN: 978-0-2412-2514-1

Printed and bound in China by L. Rex Printing Co. Ltd.

A WORLD OF IDEAS:
SEE ALL THERE IS TO KNOW

www.dk.com

What makes up a Scratch project?

Here's a Scratch project. Think of it like a play.
The action takes place in an area called the stage.
The "actors" (the sprites) are controlled by lists of
instructions (the scripts). Behind is the backdrop
– the "scenery", which can be changed.

Shark patrol
by abcd (unshared)

Click the green flag
to run (start) a
program

Backdrop
(background
picture)

Click the red
button to stop
a program

Add a script to
make the shark
sprite move

Sprites are used
for all the objects
we want to move
or control

This is the
stage

when ☐ clicked

forever

next costume

wait (0.25) secs

move (10) steps

if on edge, bounce

Scripts for sprites

This is an example of a script. It makes the shark
sprite bounce around the stage, opening and
closing its mouth. Each block gives an instruction
to the sprite. A block might tell a sprite to move,
change how it looks, talk in speech bubbles, react
to other sprites, or make a sound.

Show what you know

Fill in the spaces to practise the key language of Scratch.

1. A .... is a set of instructions (program) in Scratch.

2. Objects that perform actions in a project are called ....

3. In a Scratch program, the action takes place on the ....

4. Starting a program is called .... it.

5. A collection of sounds or graphics is called a ....

Getting Scratch

You can code online at the Scratch website, but if you aren't always connected to the internet you can install it on your computer. Ask a grown-up to help you. **You will need the newer Scratch 2.0 for this book, not the old Scratch 1.4.**

What you'll learn:
• You need Scratch 2.0
• How to use Scratch on a computer
• How to join the Scratch website
• How to save your projects

Using Scratch online.

If you register for a Scratch account, you will be able to save your projects online and share them with friends.

1 **Sign up for Scratch**
Go to **scratch.mit.edu** and select **Join Scratch** for instructions on how to register. You will need to get permission from an adult with an email address.

2 **Create in Scratch**
When you want to use Scratch, go to the Scratch website and click on **Create**. This will open the Scratch editor window.

Click on this file to see your saved projects

3 **Save in Scratch**
Projects save automatically if you're logged in to your Scratch account. You can see your saved projects by clicking on the file with an **"S"** at the top right of the screen.

S

Top tip from Scratch Cat

Need to "right click" but only have one button on your mouse? Usually you can hold down the **CTRL** key on the keyboard as you click. Not working? Then ask the owner of the computer.

Installing Scratch on a computer

If you don't have access to the internet or you want to work offline, you'll need the Scratch installer. Go to **scratch.mit.edu/scratch2download** and just follow the installation instructions.

To start Scratch, just double-click the **Scratch 2.0** icon on your desktop.

Double-click
the **Scratch 2.0**
icon to start

Operating Systems

Check that your computer's operating system is able to run Scratch.

● The online version of Scratch 2.0 will run on Windows (PC), OS X (Macs), and some Linux computers.

● The offline version might not work with some Linux computers.

● The Raspberry Pi can't run Scratch 2.0 at the moment.

You're not in this book.

Scratch online community

On the Scratch website you can share your projects and try out other coders' Scratch creations. Even better, you can explore how every project works and even change ("remix") them. Look out for the buttons shown below.

Let's explore Scratch!

See inside   Remix

Scratch tour

8

Open Scratch on your computer and this is what you'll see. All you need to create and run your Scratch projects is on this screen. Take a look around.

Experiment!
• Click the buttons and tabs to experiment with Scratch. Don't worry, you won't break the computer!

Change language

Save projects here

Delete sprite or script

Help tool

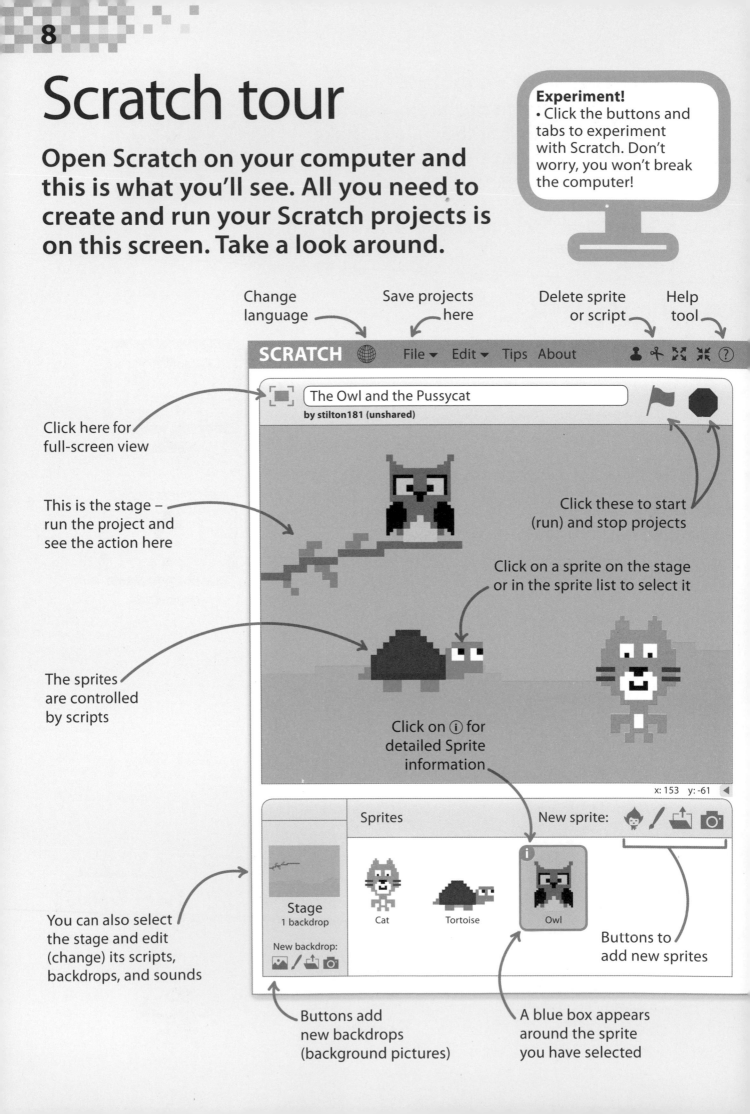

SCRATCH   File ▾   Edit ▾   Tips   About

The Owl and the Pussycat
by stilton181 (unshared)

Click here for full-screen view

This is the stage – run the project and see the action here

Click these to start (run) and stop projects

Click on a sprite on the stage or in the sprite list to select it

The sprites are controlled by scripts

Click on ⓘ for detailed Sprite information

x: 153   y: -61

Sprites

New sprite:

Stage
1 backdrop

Cat

Tortoise

Owl

New backdrop:

You can also select the stage and edit (change) its scripts, backdrops, and sounds

Buttons to add new sprites

Buttons add new backdrops (background pictures)

A blue box appears around the sprite you have selected

▶ Scratch map

The stage is where projects are run. The sprite list shows all the project's sprites. Script blocks can be found in the blocks palette. Build scripts in the scripts area.

| Stage area | Blocks palette | Scripts area |

Sprite list

Stage info

Backpack

Costumes tab – use this to change a sprite's appearance

Scripts tab

Sounds tab – use this to change the sounds a sprite makes

Click here for step-by-step guides and tips

· Saved ⬛ **stilton181** ▼

Scripts | Costumes | Sounds

Motion | Events
Looks | Control
Sound | Sensing
Pen | Operators
Data | More Blocks

Select different types of blocks

move (10) steps

turn ↻ (15) degrees

turn ↺ (15) degrees

point in direction (90 ▼)

point towards [▼]

go to x: (0) y: (0)

go to [mouse-pointer ▼]

glide (1) secs to x: (0) y: (0)

Each block is a different Scratch instruction

when [ ] clicked
forever
　go to [mouse-pointer ▼]
　move (10) steps

Blocks snap together – use the mouse to move them around

forever
　next costume
　play sound [hoot ▼] until done

These scripts control the owl sprite

x: -126
y: 96

Backpack

Backpack is used to copy sprites, costumes, scripts, and sounds between projects

Drag blocks from here into the scripts area to make scripts

Build scripts here

Your first project

Time for our first Scratch project. We're going to create some simple instructions to make the cat talk. By moving the coloured blocks around with the mouse, we can build a simple computer program called a script.

What you'll learn:
• Sprites are controlled by scripts
• How to build a script from Scratch blocks
• Things in scripts happen one block at a time from the top
• You can read Scratch to work out what it does

▶ Scratch – the friendly cat

First, open the Scratch editor: either choose **Create** on the Scratch website, or click the Scratch icon on your computer. You'll see the cat sprite standing on the stage. Let's make a script to tell the cat what to do.

Drag blocks to build a script

Click on the **Looks** label

1 Start a new script
We'll begin by getting the cat to say a friendly "Hello!" Click on the purple **Looks** label under the **Scripts** tab in the centre of the editor.

Motion	Events
Looks	Control
Sound	Sensing
Pen	Operators
Data	More Blocks

Scripts

2 Select a say block
The list of blocks in the middle of the editor will change. Click with the mouse on the top **say Hello!** block and drag it to the right, into the scripts area.

say Hello! for ② secs

3 Do it again!
Drag a second **say Hello!** block into the scripts area. Release the mouse button when the blocks overlap, so that they lock together like jigsaw pieces.

say Hello! for ② secs
say Hello! for ② secs

4 Change what the cat says
We can tell the cat to say something different. Click on the lower **say Hello!** box in the stack. Type in a new message, such as "Nice day!"

say Hello! for ② secs
say Nice day! for ② secs

New message goes here

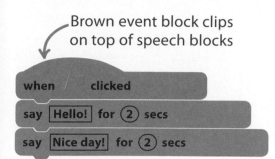

Brown event block clips on top of speech blocks

5 Completing your script

Click on the brown **Events** tab. Drag the top brown block in the list to the right, into the scripts area. Hover it over the top **say** block, then let go of the mouse button. The brown block will clip on to the two purple **say** blocks.

Clicking the flag runs the script

6 Read the whole script

The script tells us that to start things off we need to click on the green flag in the top right corner of the stage. This is called "running" the script.

Hello!

2 seconds

Nice day!

2 seconds

7 Watch the action

When you click on the flag, Scratch Cat will say "Hello!" for two seconds. Then it will say "Nice day!" for two seconds

See how the blocks work in order – the cat does each action in turn.

8 Save it!

Well done – you've built your first Scratch project! Save it by clicking on the **File** menu and choose **Save** or **Save All**.

Scratch puzzle

We've picked some blocks for our cat to try out. Draw a line from each block to the correct picture of what the cat will do.

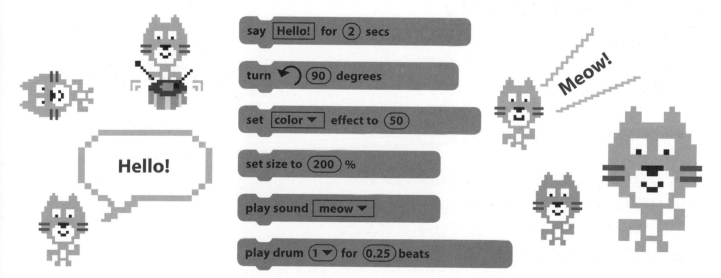

Move it!

Now for some action. Let's get our cat moving using the dark blue **Motion** blocks. Scratch measures distances in "steps". The stage is 480 steps wide and 360 steps tall. There is a useful block to stop sprites getting stuck to the walls. They just bounce off them!

What you'll learn:
• How to make a sprite move
• That Scratch measures distance in steps
• How to keep sprites the right way up

▶ Let's move the cat

Start a new project. Click on **File** above the stage and select **New**. Add this script and think about what the blocks do.

Click the green flag to run the script. The cat will move a short way to the right. Try it a few times.

Click on the **10** in the **move** block and type **100**. The cat now moves much further each time. Experiment by trying different numbers of steps.

From brown **Events** blocks

From dark blue **Motion** blocks

when   clicked

move (10) steps

10 steps

100 steps

▶ Bouncing off the walls

Now change your script to this. Read the script. What do you think it does? The **forever** block repeats the blocks inside – forever! The **if on edge, bounce** block turns the cat around at the edge of the stage.

Run the new script. The cat will now run right then left across the stage. Experiment – the more steps there are in each move, the faster the cat goes.

From yellow **Control** blocks

when   clicked

forever

move (10) steps

if on edge, bounce

The bigger this number, the faster the movement

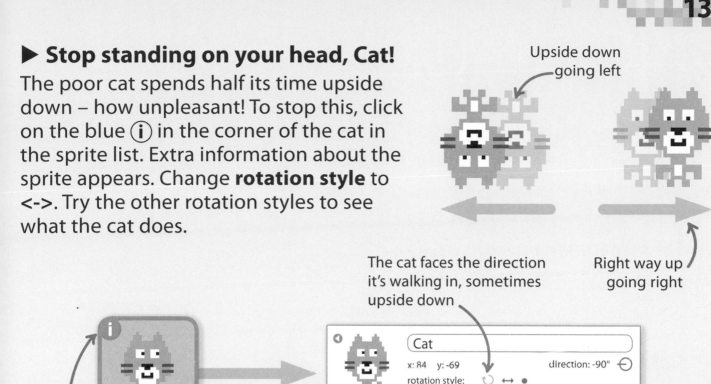

▶ Stop standing on your head, Cat!

The poor cat spends half its time upside down – how unpleasant! To stop this, click on the blue ⓘ in the corner of the cat in the sprite list. Extra information about the sprite appears. Change **rotation style** to <->. Try the other rotation styles to see what the cat does.

Upside down going left

Right way up going right

The cat faces the direction it's walking in, sometimes upside down

Cat
x: 84   y: -69   direction: -90°
rotation style:
can drag in player: ☐
show: ☑

Click here to get information about the sprite

The cat faces left or right and is always the right way up

The cat doesn't rotate at all

Show what you know
How far can you go with this quiz? All the way to the end?

1. What colour are the **Motion** blocks? ....

2. Scratch measures distances in units called ....

2a. How many of these units wide is the stage? ....

2b. How many of these units tall is the stage? ....

3. A mistake in a program is known as a "bug". This script should make the cat move across the stage slowly, but when I click the green flag to run it nothing happens! What's wrong?

forever
    move ② steps
    if on edge, bounce

....
....
....
....

We love bugs!

Which way?

When you want to move a sprite, you need to know two things: how far and which way. Every sprite has a built-in direction arrow. When a script gets to a dark blue **move** block, that's the direction in which the sprite will go.

▶ Cat follows mouse!

Let's spin our cat around in every possible direction. Open a new project in the Scratch editor. Build this script for the cat sprite. Read the script. What do you think it does? Click the green flag to see if you guessed correctly.

Move the mouse-pointer around the stage and watch the cat turn round so it always looks towards the pointer. The **forever** block runs the **point towards mouse-pointer** block over and over.

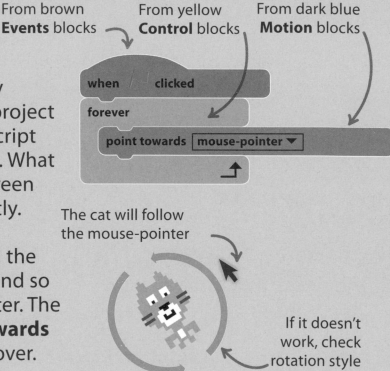

From brown **Events** blocks

From yellow **Control** blocks

From dark blue **Motion** blocks

```
when [flag] clicked
forever
    point towards [mouse-pointer ▼]
```

The cat will follow the mouse-pointer

If it doesn't work, check rotation style

◀ Sprites know where to go!

Every sprite knows what direction it's pointing. A sprite's direction is shown in the sprite information panel when you click the blue ⓘ.

As the cat spins round, you'll see its direction value change and the blue line pointer move around the direction circle.

Use the "compass" shown here to decode the direction number.

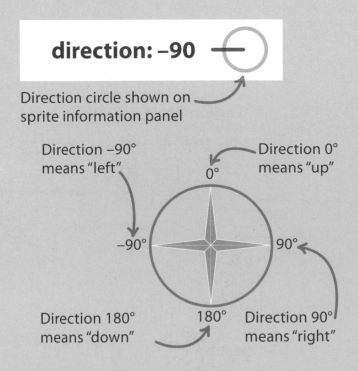

direction: –90 ⊖

Direction circle shown on sprite information panel

Direction –90° means "left"

Direction 0° means "up"

0°

–90°

90°

180°

Direction 180° means "down"

Direction 90° means "right"

▶ Choosing a sprite's direction

We can also set a sprite's direction using the window on the **point in direction** block. You can click on the little triangle beside the number for useful directions, or just click on the window and type in a number.

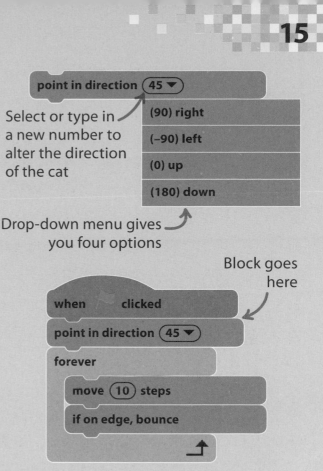

Select or type in a new number to alter the direction of the cat

Drop-down menu gives you four options

▶ Bouncing off the walls again

Add the **point in direction 45** block to the "bouncing off the walls" script from page 12. Put it after the **when green flag clicked** block but before the **forever** block. Run the script. The cat will set off diagonally. Try using different directions and rotation styles.

Show what you know
Know your way around Scratch? Then try these brain-teasers!

1. What number should replace the **?** in this block to set the sprite's direction to:

`point in direction ( ? ▼ )`

Up = ... Left = ...

Down = ... Right = ...

2. Test your Scratch script reading powers! What does this script do? Read it carefully and try to act each block out in your mind

....

....

....

....

....

Loops

In computer programs, we often want to carry out the same instructions more than once. To avoid having to put down the same blocks many times, we can wrap them in a loop instruction that repeats the blocks. Meet **forever** and **repeat** loops!

What you'll learn:
• How to repeat a group of blocks using a loop
• The difference between **forever** and **repeat** loops
• How to make some noise in Scratch

▶ Running down the blocks

Start a new project and make this script. Read, understand, and run it. It runs very quickly and doesn't do much.

When we run the script, each block is run in turn from top to bottom. First the cat turns a little, then the cat's colour changes to green.

Blocks run in this order

when ⚐ clicked
turn ↻ (15) degrees
change [color ▼] effect by (25)

I feel a bit off-colour!

▶ Forever loops

A loop instruction runs a script in the normal order from top to bottom, but then loops back to the top. The loop runs the blocks inside over and over again. Try wrapping a **forever** loop around the blocks from the last script.

Now the cat turns more and changes colour each time the blocks in the **forever** loop are repeated.

Press the red button to stop the loop.

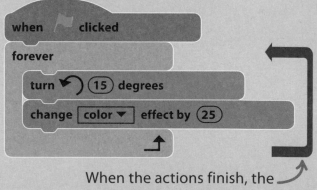

when ⚐ clicked
forever
turn ↻ (15) degrees
change [color ▼] effect by (25)

When the actions finish, the program always goes back to the start of the loop

The red button stops a program

Help! I'm in a spin!

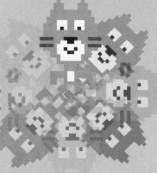

▶ Repeat loops

If we want to repeat a group of blocks only a few times and then get on with the rest of the script, we can use the **repeat** loop block.

Try this script for a siren that annoys the cat. The **repeat** loop runs the two **play note** blocks 10 times and only then runs the **think** block. Try changing the number of repeats.

Selects buzzing

From pink
Sound
blocks

```
when    clicked
set instrument to (20▼)
repeat (10)
    play note (64 ▼) for (0.5) beats
    play note (60 ▼) for (0.5) beats
think  Noisy!
```

Finished

Script goes back to the start of the loop, running the blocks inside 10 times

That really is noisy!

You're not kidding!

Show what you know
What do you know about loops? Test yourself with this quiz.

1. Loops are used to .... groups of blocks.

2. Two types of scratch loops are .... and ....

3. You can stop a **forever** loop by clicking the ....

4. In which section do you find the pink blocks? ....

5. Which block section has the loops in? ....

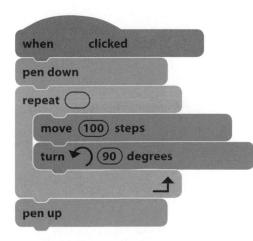

```
when    clicked
pen down
repeat ( )
    move (100) steps
    turn ↰ (90) degrees
pen up
```

6. Bug hunt! This script should draw the four sides of a square, but nothing happens when it's run. Can you spot and suggest a fix for the bug? Programmers call this "debugging".

....

....

....

Animation

The characters in cartoons seem to move, but really you are just watching lots of slightly different pictures that fool your brain into seeing movement. This is called animation. Sprites can be animated in the same way.

What you'll learn:
• How to animate sprites
• Sprites can change how they look
• How to use costumes
• How to load new sprites from the Scratch library

▶ Changing costumes

Our cat sprite has two different pictures, or "costumes", it can show. Start a new scratch project and click on the **Costumes** tab just above the block list. You will then see the two costumes the cat sprite can "wear".

▼ Walking the cat

To animate the cat, build and run this script. The **forever** loop repeats the **next costume** block. The picture of the sprite changes every half second, and this makes the cat look like it's walking. Try adding a **move** block in the loop to improve the animation.

Costumes tab

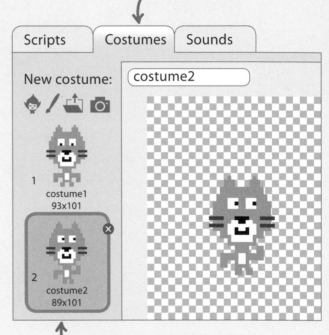

Scripts   Costumes   Sounds

New costume:

costume2

1   costume1
    93x101

2   costume2
    89x101

Sprite's costumes are listed in order

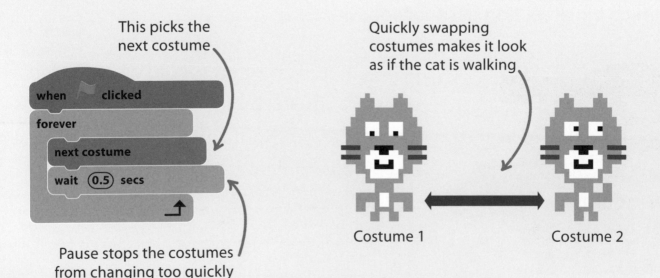

This picks the next costume

when 🏳 clicked
forever
    next costume
    wait (0.5) secs

Pause stops the costumes from changing too quickly

Quickly swapping costumes makes it look as if the cat is walking

Costume 1   Costume 2

▶ Dancing ballerina

You can use this same script to get other sprites dancing! Let's add the ballerina sprite to the project. Click on **Choose sprite from library** at the top of the sprite list. Then select the ballerina and click **OK**.

Add the costume-changing script to the ballerina's scripts area. She has four costumes. Click on the **Costumes** tab to see them. When you run the script, she uses them all as she dances on the stage.

New sprite:

Choose sprite from library

Click on the first icon to see all the sprites

Look! I'm dancing!

Let's have a party!

◀ Sprite party!

Try adding lots of dancing sprites to your project. Choose sprites with two or more costumes. Try Dinosaur1 or some of the dancing kids.

Show what you know
You can make sprites dance. Can you solve these problems too?

1. A different picture a sprite can show on the stage is a ....

2. .... is showing pictures with slight differences in order to make a sprite appear to move.

3. Can you rearrange the sprites below to animate a jumping pony? Write the numbers 1 to 5 in the boxes to show the correct order.

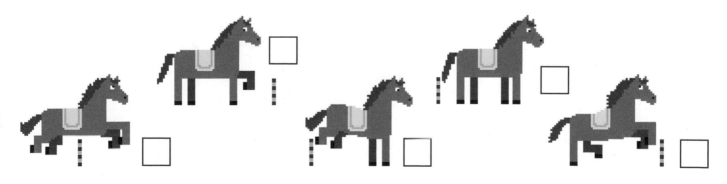

Party time!

We've learned a lot about making sprites do things, but a project isn't complete if it happens on a silent, white stage! Let's see how to give a project some scenery and music from the Scratch libraries to liven things up.

What you'll learn:
• How to change the background picture
• How to add effects to the backdrop
• How to add music to your project

"party" stage

▶ Adding scenery – backdrops

Just as a sprite can have many costumes, the stage too can have more than one background picture, or backdrop. Click on the **Add new backdrop from library** button at the bottom left of the **Stage info** area.

It's Scratch Cat's birthday, so choose the "party" stage. You'll see the cat on the stage! You can load more than one backdrop. Try loading "underwater2".

You can switch backdrop in any script using the **switch backdrop** or **next backdrop** blocks from the **Looks** section.

"underwater2" stage

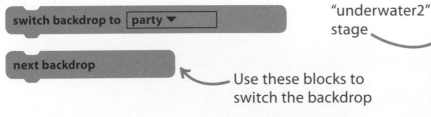

Use these blocks to switch the backdrop

▶ Lightshow!

We can add scripts to the stage: click on the small picture of the stage area at the top of the **Stage info** area. Then try running this script with your party backdrop to bring it to life.

Continually changes the colour of the stage

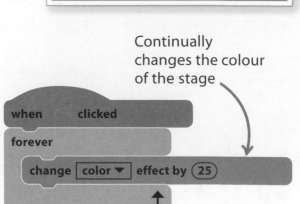

▶ Music

A party isn't a party without music!
Sounds can be loaded into a sprite or
the stage. But you must make scripts
to play them in the **Scripts area**.

Clicking on the speaker under
the **Sounds** tab willl take you
to the **Sound Library**

 Load some music
Click on the stage again. Then click
on the **Sounds** tab above the blocks and
select **Choose sound from library** (the
speaker symbol).

Choose your groove!

Plays the whole
sound before going
to the next block

2 **Select a tune**
Choose one of the music loops, such
as "dance funky", and click **OK** in the bottom
right corner to load. The sound will appear
on the list of sounds.

3 **Make, read, and run a script**
Click on the **Scripts** tab and make
this script. Read the script and run it.
You should have never-ending music!

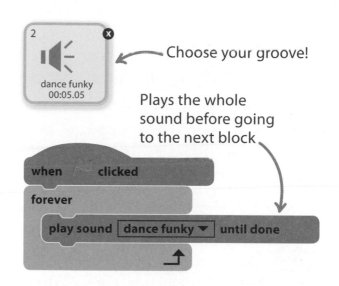

Show what you know

The cat's in the mood for a party. Are you in the mood for a quiz?

1. A background picture on the stage is called a ....

2. Circle the block that plays a whole sound before carrying on:

play sound pop ▼   play sound pop ▼ until done

3. True or false?

a. A project can have only one backdrop loaded. ....

b. Only the sprite that loaded a sound can play it. ....

c. The stage can have sounds and scripts. ....

d. Once you've chosen a backdrop for a script you can't change it. ....

e. A sprite can use a script to change the stage's backdrop. ....

if-then

If it's raining, we decide to wear a raincoat. We can make this kind of decision in Scratch using the **if-then** blocks from the yellow **Control** section. Like loops, they wrap around other blocks and control when they are run.

Spin control

Let's use **if-then** blocks to decide when our cat spins. We'll use some light blue **Sensing** blocks, which ask a "true or false?" question. Find them under the **Scripts** tab.

Sensing block goes into window at top of **if-then** block

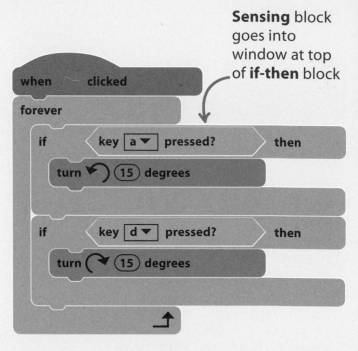

1 Start a new project
Add this script. What do you think it does? The block inside each **if-then** block is only run if the answer to the question at the top of the block is "true".

Cat turns 15 degrees to the left

a =

2 Run the script
What happens? Nothing! Press the **"a"** key and the cat turns backwards. Let the key go and it stops. The **turn** block inside the first **if-then** block is only run when the answer to the question **key a pressed?** is "true".

Cat turns 15 to the right

3 Now press the "d" key
The cat turns the other way. The **turn** block inside the second **if-then** block is only run when the answer to the question **key d pressed?** is "true". If neither key is pressed, then both **turn** blocks are skipped.

d =

A closer look at the if-then block

Look at this **if-then** block taken from a script.
Read it carefully and think about what it does.

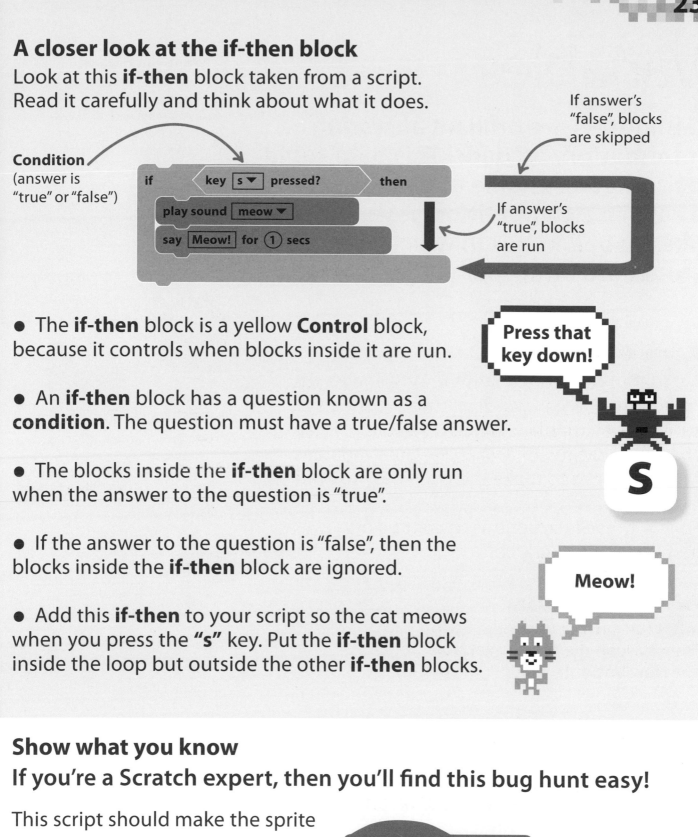

If answer's "false", blocks are skipped

Condition (answer is "true" or "false")

If answer's "true", blocks are run

- The **if-then** block is a yellow **Control** block, because it controls when blocks inside it are run.

- An **if-then** block has a question known as a **condition**. The question must have a true/false answer.

- The blocks inside the **if-then** block are only run when the answer to the question is "true".

- If the answer to the question is "false", then the blocks inside the **if-then** block are ignored.

- Add this **if-then** to your script so the cat meows when you press the **"s"** key. Put the **if-then** block inside the loop but outside the other **if-then** blocks.

Press that key down!

S

Meow!

Show what you know

If you're a Scratch expert, then you'll find this bug hunt easy!

This script should make the sprite change colour when you press the space key, but the sprite changes colour all the time. Can you spot the "bug"? ....
....
....

Variables

Computers are brilliant at storing information, or "data". This data could be someone's name or the weight of a cake in a competition. A variable is like a labelled box in which you can store data until your program needs it.

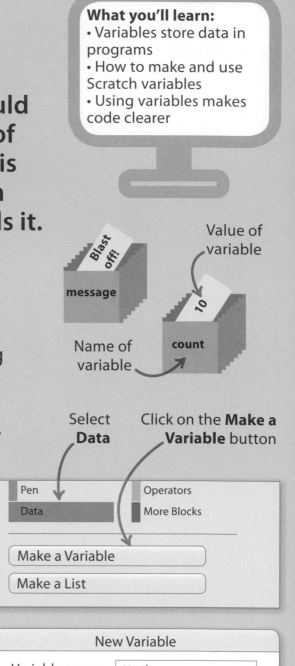

Value of variable

Name of variable

count

message

A box with a label

A variable can store a number or some words (programmers call words a "string"). The thing stored in a variable is called its value. You can change the value of a variable. Give variables helpful names to make the code easy to read.

Follow these instructions to create your first variable in Scratch.

Select **Data**

Click on the **Make a Variable** button

Pen	Operators
Data	More Blocks

Make a Variable

Make a List

1 **Start with Data**
Select **Data** under the **Scripts** tab. Then click on the **Make a Variable** button. The **New Variable** window will pop-up.

New Variable

Variable name: count

● For all sprites   ○ For this sprite only
☐ Cloud variable (stored on server)

OK   Cancel

2 **Name it, check it, click it!**
First, give your variable a useful name. Check **For all sprites**, and click **OK**. (You can ignore the **For this sprite only** and **Cloud variable** boxes.)

Tick to show the variable on the stage

The variable block can be used inside other blocks

3 **Get to know your blocks!**
Blocks for this variable will then appear in the blocks area. Make sure you know what each of the blocks does.

☑ count

This block gives the variable a value

set count ▼ to 0

Increase the variable's value using this block (a negative number decreases the value)

change count ▼ by ①

► Countdown cat

Time to see some variables in action. Start a new project.

In the orange **Data** section, create two variables called **count** and **message**. Always give your variables names that explain what's stored in them.

Add this script. Make sure you drag the little orange blocks with **count** and **message** on them into the windows of the **say** blocks. Don't type the words into the **say** block windows. If you do, the cat will say the variable's name rather than what's stored in the variable.

Read the script. Can you work out what's going to happen? Now run the script.

Experiment with the numbers and text in the script. Can you make the cat count up instead of down?

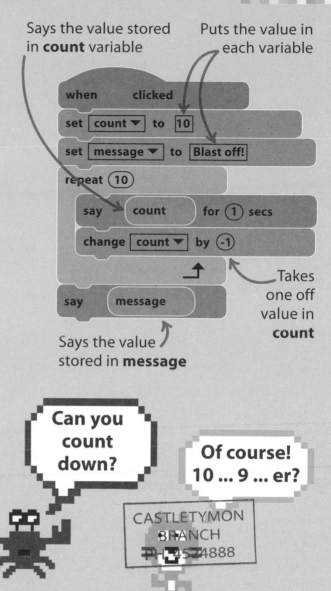

Says the value stored in **count** variable

Puts the value in each variable

Says the value stored in **message**

Takes one off value in **count**

Can you count down?

Of course! 10 ... 9 ... er?

CASTLETYMON BRANCH PH: 4524888

Show what you know
Test how much Scratch data you've stored in your brain-box.

1. A variable has a name and a ....

2. **Make a Variable** button is found in the orange .... blocks section.

3. Fill in the speech bubbles for these sets of blocks:

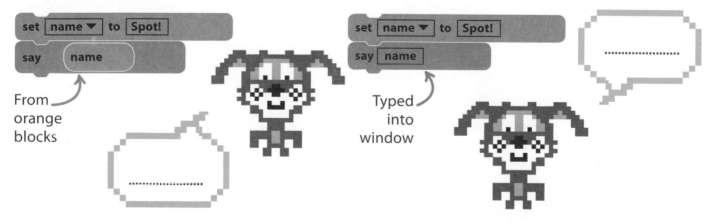

From orange blocks

Typed into window

Maths

Scratch can do all the maths you know about. But some of the symbols it uses are different, to fit with what's on your computer's keyboard. We can do sums in Scratch and use variables in them. Scratch can even roll a dice for us.

What you'll learn:
• How to do maths in Scratch
• What maths symbols computers use
• How to do sums with variables
• How to "roll dice" using the computer

▶ Maths tools

To do maths you need the green **Operators** blocks. Each block does a different sum with the numbers in the two windows.

▼ Placing operators

Wherever you put an **operator** block, it will put the answer to the sum. So if you put it into the window of a **say** block, the cat will say the answer.

Add (+)

⑦ + ㉒

The "+" block adds the two numbers in the block together.

Subtract (−)

㉔ − ㉘

The "−" block takes the second number away from the first.

Multiply (*)

⑪ * ⑩

Scratch uses the "*" symbol, because "x" looks like a letter.

Divide (/)

⑫⓪ / ④

The keyboard has no division sign. Scratch uses "/" instead.

say   ⑫ + ⑤

Add (+) block put into **say** window

17

Answer

Clever cat!

▶ Maths and variables

We can use **operator** blocks to do sums with variables. For example, to find the total number of pets we can use the **add (+)** block to add up the values of the variables **dogs** and **cats**, and store the answer in a variable called **pets**.

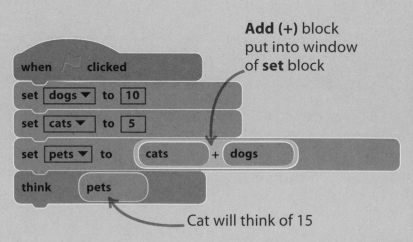

Add (+) block put into window of **set** block

when 🏳 clicked

set dogs ▼ to 10

set cats ▼ to 5

set pets ▼ to (cats + dogs)

think   pets

Cat will think of 15

▶ Throwing dice

A random number is one that we can't predict. It's like a number we get when we roll a dice – we don't know what the number will be before we roll. Scratch can act like a dice and "roll" for us. Try this script in a new project.

Read the script, then run it. The cat will show you 4 random numbers as it thinks of them. Random numbers are useful in games, because they make the action difficult to guess.

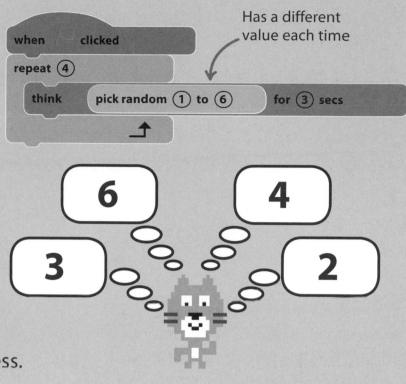

Has a different value each time

Show what you know

Have a go at these mathematical mind-bogglers.

1. You are the computer! Calculate the values of these blocks.

3 + 10   8 + 11   12 – 8   22 – 11   5 * 6   9 / 3

....

2. These blocks use variables in their sums. Can you work out the answers?

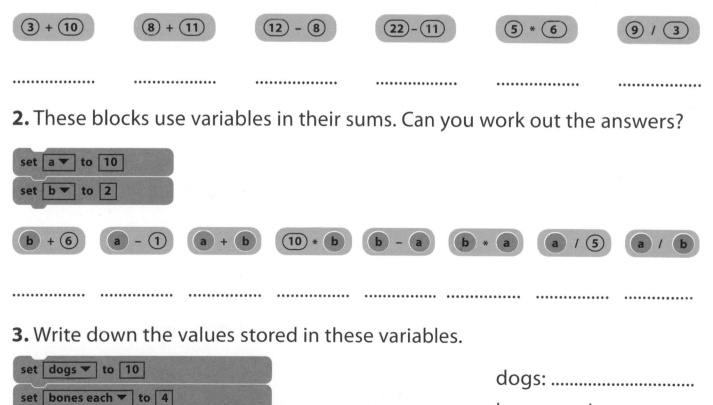

set a ▼ to 10
set b ▼ to 2

b + 6   a – 1   a + b   10 * b   b – a   b * a   a / 5   a / b

....

3. Write down the values stored in these variables.

set dogs ▼ to 10
set bones each ▼ to 4
set total bones ▼ to   dogs   *   bones each

dogs: ....

bones each: ....

total bones: ....

Inputs and events

The data put into a program, such as the answer you type when Scratch asks a question, is called input. Events are actions, like clicking a sprite or pressing a chosen key, that Scratch can use to run scripts.

What you'll learn:
• How to ask questions and use the answers
• What an **Event** block is
• How to run a script with a key press or click

The cat asks the question

What's for lunch?

You type in "Cat food"

Cat food!

Then press **enter** or click the blue tick

▼ Just ask

Sprites can use questions and answers using the light blue **ask** and **answer** blocks under the **Sensing** tab. Start a new project and add this script. Read the script. What do you think it does? Run the script to test your ideas.

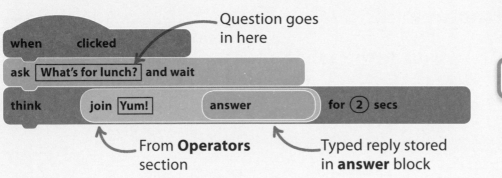

Question goes in here

when clicked

ask What's for lunch? and wait

think join Yum! answer for 2 secs

From **Operators** section

Typed reply stored in **answer** block

Dinner time for Scratch Cat!

The cat asks the question and waits for you to type in your reply using the keyboard. When you press **enter**, what you typed in becomes the value of the **answer** block.

Yum! Cat food!

Answers are like variables

The **answer** block works just like a variable. Wherever you put the **answer** block it will be replaced by your answer to the question. The green **join** block in the script above just takes what's in its two windows and links them together as a single item.

He's always hungry!

▶ Events trigger scripts

Events are things that happen that the computer can tell Scratch about, such as key presses and mouse clicks. The brown **Events** "header" blocks start to run a script when a chosen event happens, in the same way that the green flag button can start a script when you click on it.

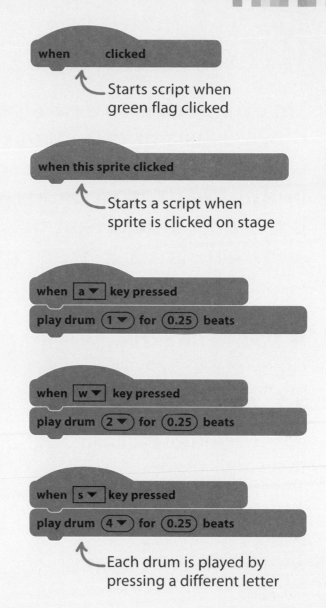

when ⚑ clicked — Starts script when green flag clicked

when this sprite clicked — Starts a script when sprite is clicked on stage

▶ Build a drum-kit

Create lots of scripts like these. Select a different key and a different drum for each version of the script. The blocks below an **Events** header are run when you press the correct key. Play an epic drum solo using your selected keys!

when a ▼ key pressed
play drum 1 ▼ for 0.25 beats

when w ▼ key pressed
play drum 2 ▼ for 0.25 beats

when s ▼ key pressed
play drum 4 ▼ for 0.25 beats — Each drum is played by pressing a different letter

What a racket!

Show what you know

Can you answer these questions about inputs and events?

1. Which blue **Sensing** block makes a sprite ask a question? ....

2. Which block holds the reply given to the question? ....

3. Something that happens to the computer, like a mouse click or a key press, is called an ....

4. What happens if I click a sprite with this script?

....

....

when this sprite clicked
say You clicked me!

5. Can more than one script be running at once? ....

if-then-else

Let's meet the **if-then-else** block. This block uses a question, or **condition**, to choose between two groups of blocks to run. We'll also look at some handy **condition** blocks that use variables and values to ask "true or false?"

▶ Comparing things

There is another kind of block that asks a "true or false?" question. In the green **Operators** section there are 3 blocks that compare what's in their two windows. To read them, you need to know what these symbols mean: =, <, and >.

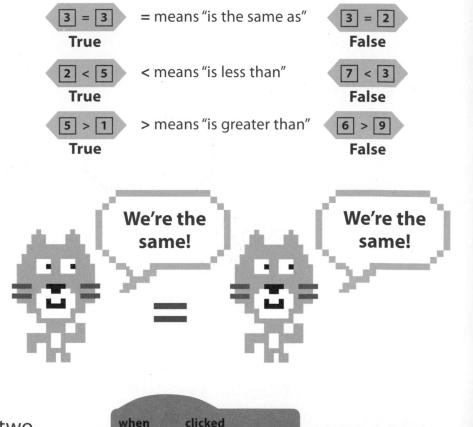

3 = 3 **True**	= means "is the same as"	3 = 2 **False**
2 < 5 **True**	< means "is less than"	7 < 3 **False**
5 > 1 **True**	> means "is greater than"	6 > 9 **False**

We're the same!

We're the same!

▶ Password checker

An **if-then-else** block has two groups of blocks inside. It runs the first group if the condition is true, and the second group if the condition is false. We can use it to check a password.

when ⚑ clicked

ask `Password?` and wait

if ⟨ answer = `dragon` ⟩ then

say `Enter friend!`

else

say `Go away!`

Block runs if answer is "dragon"

Block runs if answer is NOT "dragon"

Equals (=) block compares answer with password

▶ Friend or foe?

Read and run the script. Only one of the two **say** blocks is run, the other is skipped. We get just one of the replies. If we type in the correct password, the cat greets us. Otherwise ("else") we're sent away.

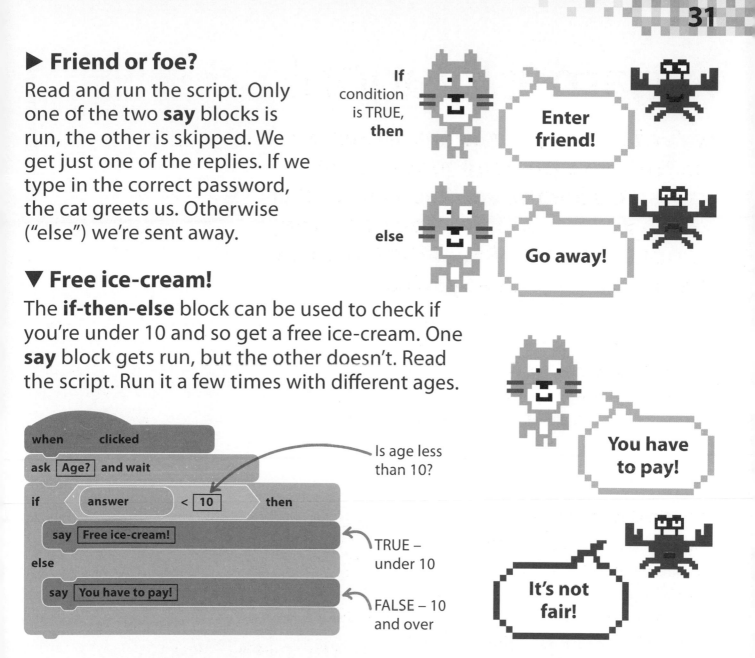

If condition is TRUE, **then**

Enter friend!

else

Go away!

▼ Free ice-cream!

The **if-then-else** block can be used to check if you're under 10 and so get a free ice-cream. One **say** block gets run, but the other doesn't. Read the script. Run it a few times with different ages.

You have to pay!

```
when        clicked
ask  Age?  and wait
if         answer     < 10      then
    say  Free ice-cream!
else
    say  You have to pay!
```

Is age less than 10?

TRUE – under 10

FALSE – 10 and over

It's not fair!

Show what you know

Answer the questions to prove you're a smooth Scratch operator!

1. What shape blocks go into the **condition** window of an **if-then** or **if-then-else** block?

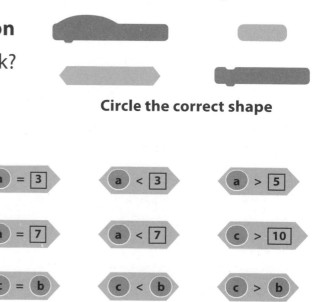

Circle the correct shape

2. Look at the variables below, then circle the green operator blocks that have the value "true".

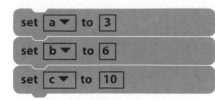

```
set  a ▼  to  3
set  b ▼  to  6
set  c ▼  to  10
```

a = 3	a < 3	a > 5
a = 7	a < 7	c > 10
c = b	c < b	c > b

A game: Dragon!

We've learned a lot about Scratch so far. Now let's put it all together into a game. You are the cat. You can control where you are on the stage using the computer mouse. Avoid the ferocious dragon for as long as you can!

What you'll learn:
• How we put a game together from sprites and scripts
• How to detect when two sprites touch
• How a script can stop a project

▶ Enter the dragon

Add the "Dragon" sprite to the project. Add a variable for all sprites, and give it the name **speed**.

Leave this box ticked

☑ speed

Dragon

▶ Get the dragon bouncing

Choose the dragon in the sprite list and add this script. This is the bouncing script we used before, but with a slight change. We control the dragon's speed with a variable and set the dragon off in a different direction each game. Read and run the script. The dragon bounces around the stage.

```
when      clicked
set  speed ▼  to 10
point towards  mouse-pointer ▼
forever
    move    speed   steps
    if on edge, bounce
```

Points dragon in a new direction when run

▶ Mouse controls cat!

Now select the cat in the sprite list and add this script. Carefully read the script. It "sticks" the cat to the mouse-pointer. Inside the loop it also checks if we're touching the dragon. If we are, it stops the project – game over! Run the script to check that it works.

```
when      clicked
wait ① secs
forever
    go to  mouse-pointer ▼
    if        touching  Dragon ▼ ?        then
        stop  all ▼
```

wait block lets dragon move away

If true, then all scripts stop

▶ Score

A proper game needs a score and a challenge. Add a new variable for all sprites called **score**. Leave it ticked so that it shows on the stage.

Add this script to the cat. Read it. For every 3 seconds you avoid the dragon, you score a point. But every time you score, the dragon's speed goes up one!

Run the game to see that it works as you expect. If it doesn't, check everything from the beginning. Now compete with your friends to get the best score. Why not add a backdrop and some music?

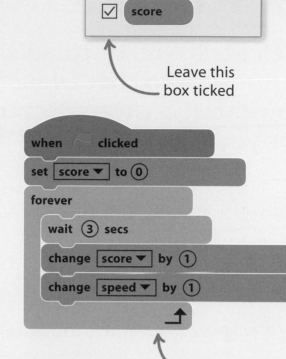

Leave this box ticked

The more you score, the faster the dragon moves

Do you like Scratch?

Only when I itch!

Show what you know
Answer the quiz - will it be a high score or "game over"?

1. Why do we leave the check box on the **score** variable ticked?

....

2. How could you make the dragon go at half speed at the start?

....

3. Which block could you add inside the cat's **forever** loop to make it look like it's walking? ....

4. How many costumes does the dragon have? ....

5. What would happen if you right-clicked the dragon on the sprite list and chose **duplicate**? ....

....

Solutions

Well done, you've completed all the tasks! Time to check your "Show what you know" answers. How did you do? Are you a Scratch genius now?

pages 4–5 What is Scratch?

1. A **script** is a set of instructions (program) in Scratch.

2. Objects that perform actions in a project are called **sprites**.

3. In a Scratch program, the action takes place on the **stage**.

4. Starting a program is called **running** it.

5. A collection of sounds or graphics is called a **library**.

pages 10–11 Your first project

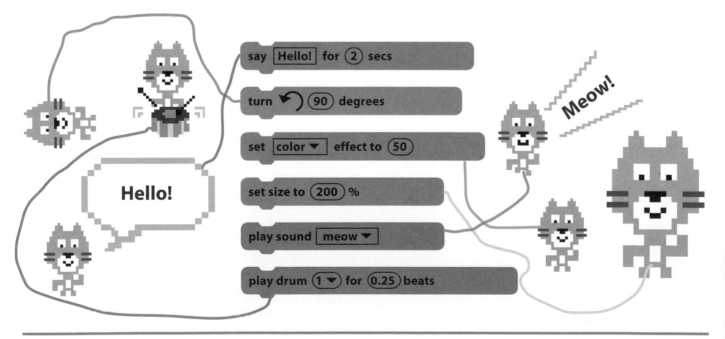

pages 12–13 Move it!

1. What colour are the **Motion** blocks? **dark blue**

2. Scratch measures distances in units called **steps**.

2a. How many of these units wide is the stage?

480

2b. How many of these units tall is the stage?

360

3. A mistake in a program is known as a "bug". This script should make the cat move across the stage slowly, but when I click the green flag to run it nothing happens! What's wrong?

The "when green flag clicked" block is missing.

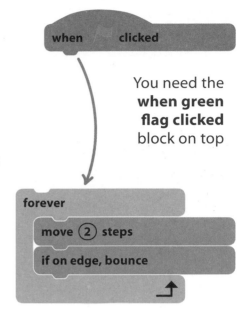

You need the **when green flag clicked** block on top

---

pages 14–15 Which way?

1. What number should replace the **?** in this block to set the sprite's direction to:

Up = **0**   Left = **–90**

Down = **180**   Right = **90**

2. Test your Scratch script reading powers! What does this script do? Read it carefully and try to act each block out in your mind.

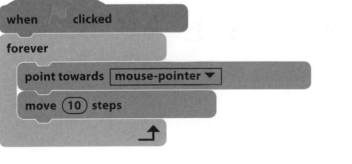

The script makes the cat run towards the mouse-pointer on the stage.

---

pages 16–17 Loops

1. Loops are used to **repeat** groups of blocks.

2. Two types of Scratch loops are **forever** and **repeat**.

3. You can stop a **forever** loop by clicking the **red button**.

4. In which section do you find the pink blocks? **Sound**

5. Which block section has the loops in? **Control**

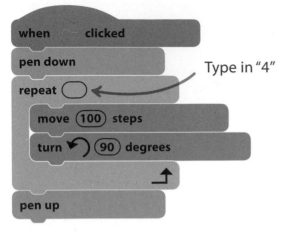

Type in "4"

6. Bug hunt! This script should draw the four sides of a square, but nothing happens when it's run. Can you spot and suggest a fix for the bug? Programmers call this "debugging".

The repeat loop doesn't say how many repeats to do. Type "4" into its window to fix the bug.

---

pages 18–19 Animation

1. A different picture a sprite can show on the stage is a **costume**.

2. Animation is showing pictures with slight differences in order to make a sprite appear to move.

3. Can you rearrange the sprites below to animate a jumping pony? Write the numbers 1 to 5 in the boxes to show the correct order.

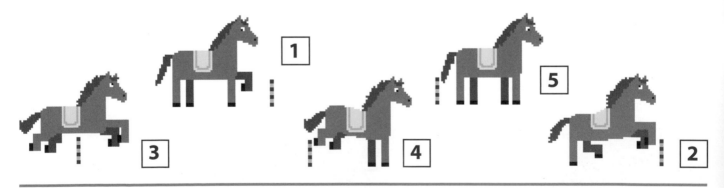

---

pages 20–21 Party time!

1. A background picture on the stage is called a **backdrop**.

2. Circle the block that plays a whole sound before carrying on:

3. True or false?

a. A project can have only one backdrop loaded. **False**

b. Only the sprite that loaded a sound can play it. **True**

c. The stage can have sounds and scripts. **True**

d. Once you've chosen a backdrop for a script you can't change it. **False**

e. A sprite can use a script to change the stage's backdrop. **True**

---

pages 22–23 if-then

This script should make the sprite change color when you press the space key, but the sprite changes color all the time. Can you spot the "bug"? **The "change color effect by 25" block needs to go inside the "if-then" block.**

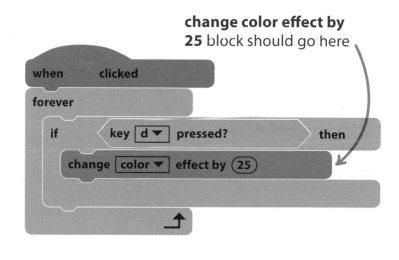

change color effect by 25 block should go here

---

pages 24–25 Variables

1. A variable has a name and a **value**.

2. Make a Variable button is found in the orange **Data** blocks section.

3. Fill in the speech bubbles for these sets of blocks:

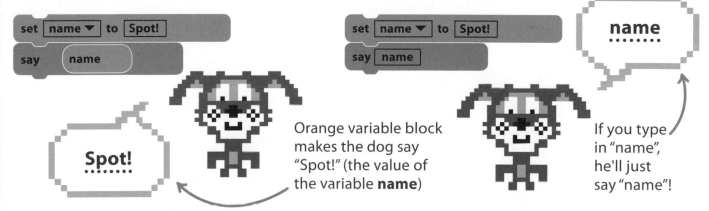

Orange variable block makes the dog say "Spot!" (the value of the variable **name**)

Spot!

name

If you type in "name", he'll just say "name"!

(Always use the orange variable block to get a variable's value.)

pages 26–27 Maths

1. You are the computer! Calculate the values of these blocks.

(3) + (10) (8) + (11) (12) – (8) (22) – (11) (5) * (6) (9) / (3)

13 **19** **4** **11** **30** **3**

2. These blocks use variables in their sums. Can you work out the answers?

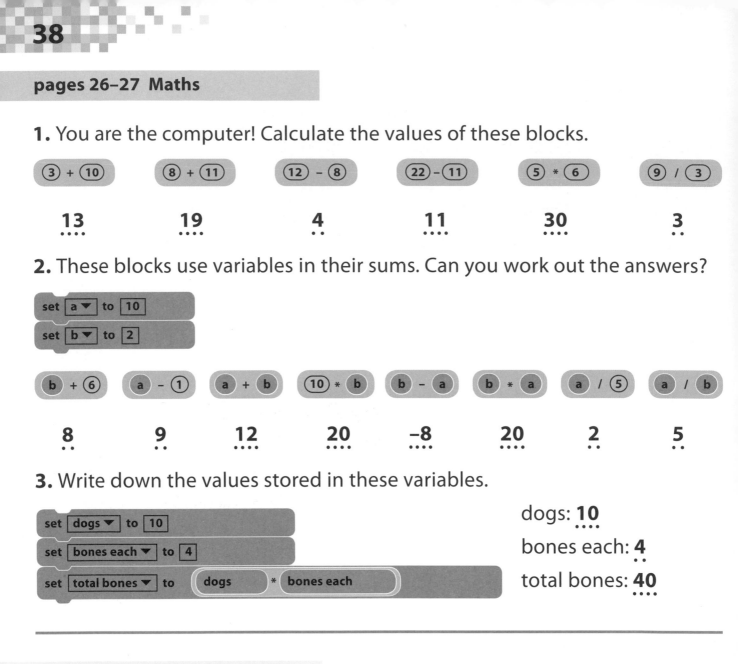

set a ▼ to 10
set b ▼ to 2

(b) + (6) (a) – (1) (a) + (b) (10) * (b) (b) – (a) (b) * (a) (a) / (5) (a) / (b)

8 **9** **12** **20** **–8** **20** **2** **5**

3. Write down the values stored in these variables.

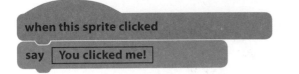

set dogs ▼ to 10
set bones each ▼ to 4
set total bones ▼ to (dogs * bones each)

dogs: **10**
bones each: **4**
total bones: **40**

---

pages 28–29 Input and events

1. Which blue **Sensing** block makes a sprite ask a question? **ask**

2. Which block holds the reply given to the question? **answer**

3. Something that happens to the computer, like a mouse click or a key press, is called an **event**.

4. What happens if I click a sprite with this script?

when this sprite clicked
say You clicked me!

The sprite says: "You clicked me!"

5. Can more than one script be running at once? **Yes. (Many scripts can run on many sprites – all at once.)**

pages 30–31 if-then-else

1. What shape blocks go into the **condition** window of an **if-then** or **if-then-else** block?

Circle the correct shape

2. Look at the variables below, then circle the green operator blocks that have the value "true".

set [a ▼] to [3]
set [b ▼] to [6]
set [c ▼] to [10]

a = 3   a < 3   a > 5
a = 7   a < 7   c > 10
c = b   c < b   c > b

---

pages 32–33 A game: Dragon!

1. Why do we leave the check box on the **score** variable ticked?
The box is ticked so the score is shown on the stage.

2. How could you make the dragon go at half speed at the start?
Change "set speed 10" to "set speed 5".

3. Which block could you add inside the cat's **forever** loop to make it look like it's walking? **The "next costume" block from "Looks".**

4. How many costumes does the dragon have? **2 (You might want to try altering the game script so that the dragon changes costumes when it touches the cat.)**

5. What would happen if you right-clicked the dragon on the sprite list and chose **duplicate**?
You'd find yourself being chased by TWO dragons, and that would make the game very hard!

Glossary

Stuck in Scratch? Click on **Tips** on the menu bar for advice. Or use the **Help tool** (?) – click on it, and then click on a block to bring up the help page for that block.

animation
Changing pictures quickly to make something appear to move on the screen.

backdrop
The picture behind the sprites on the stage.

backpack
A way to copy things between Scratch projects.

block
An instruction in Scratch. Blocks can be joined together.

bug
A mistake in a program. It's called a bug because insects got into the wiring of the first computers, causing errors.

condition
A "true or false?" question that is used to make a decision in a computer program.

costume
The picture a sprite shows on the stage.

data
Information – for example, numbers or words.

debug
To remove bugs; to find and fix the errors in a program.

event
Something that happens on the computer, like a mouse click.

input
Data that goes into a program; for example, from the keyboard.

library
A collection of sprites, sounds, or costumes.

loop
An instruction that makes other instructions repeat.

program
A list of instructions that tell a computer what to do.

operator
A block that works something out from data, such as adding two numbers together.

operating system (OS)
The program that controls everything on your computer, such as OS X or Windows.

run
To start a program.

script
A stack of instructions that are run in order.

sprite
A picture on the stage that a script can move and change.

stage
The area containing the sprites, where a Scratch project runs.

string
The word used by programmers for data that contains words.

variable
A place to store data in a program. A variable always has a name and a value.

Note for parents

Help your child work logically through any difficulties. Check for obvious errors, such as swapping similar blocks in scripts. Also check that scripts are controlling the correct sprites. Don't forget that using Scratch should be fun. The Scratch website is run by Massachusetts Institute of Technology (MIT) and is intended to be safe for children to use. Try it yourself!